Cobblers
crisps, pies & more

pil

Publications International, Ltd.

Pictured on the front cover: Nectarine-Raspberry Cobbler *(page 10).*
Pictured on the back cover *(left to right):* Blueberry Shortcake *(page 111)* and
Peach Turnover *(page 112).*

ISBN: 978-1-4508-9984-0

Manufactured in China.

8 7 6 5 4 3 2 1

Microwave Cooking: Microwave ovens vary in wattage. Use the cooking times as
guidelines and check for doneness before adding more time.

Preparation/Cooking Times: Preparation times are based on the approximate amount
of time required to assemble the recipe before cooking, baking, chilling or serving. These
times include preparation steps such as measuring, chopping and mixing. The fact that some
preparations and cooking can be done simultaneously is taken into account. Preparation of
optional ingredients and serving suggestions is not included.

WARNING: Food preparation, baking and cooking involve inherent dangers: misuse of
electric products, sharp electric tools, boiling water, hot stoves, allergic reactions, foodborne
illnesses and the like, pose numerous potential risks. Publications International, Ltd. (PIL)
assumes no responsibility or liability for any damages you may experience as a result of
following recipes, instructions, tips or advice in this publication.

While we hope this publication helps you find new ways to eat delicious foods, you may not
always achieve the results desired due to variations in ingredients, cooking temperatures,
typos, errors, omissions, or individual cooking abilities.

Publications International, Ltd.

Contents

Crazy for Cobblers

Pear and Cranberry Cobbler

MAKES 6 TO 8 SERVINGS

Topping

1	cup all-purpose flour
2	tablespoons sugar
2	teaspoons baking powder
¼	teaspoon salt
¼	cup (½ stick) cold butter, cut into pieces
½	cup milk

Filling

4	cups diced peeled ripe pears (3 to 4 medium pears)
2	cups fresh cranberries
½	cup sugar
3	tablespoons all-purpose flour
¼	teaspoon ground cinnamon
2	tablespoons butter, cut into pieces

1. Preheat oven to 375°F. Spray 10-inch round or oval baking dish with nonstick cooking spray.

2. Combine 1 cup flour, 2 tablespoons sugar, baking powder and salt in medium bowl. Cut in ¼ cup butter with pastry blender or two knives until mixture resembles coarse crumbs. Stir in milk until soft, sticky dough forms.

3. Combine pears, cranberries, ½ cup sugar, 3 tablespoons flour and cinnamon in large bowl; toss gently to coat. Spoon into prepared baking dish; dot with 2 tablespoons butter. Drop tablespoonfuls of dough onto filling. Place baking dish on rimmed baking sheet.

4. Bake 25 to 35 minutes or until filling is bubbly and topping is golden brown. Serve warm.

Peach & Berry Cobbler

MAKES 6 SERVINGS

Vegetable cooking spray

1 package (16 ounces) frozen peach slices

1 package (16 ounces) frozen mixed berries (strawberries, blueberries and raspberries)

1 cup V8 V-Fusion® Peach Mango Juice

1 tablespoon cornstarch

1 teaspoon almond extract

1 package (18.25 ounces) yellow cake mix

1 stick butter (4 ounces), cut into pieces

Confectioners' sugar

Slow Cooker Directions

1. Spray the inside of a 6-quart slow cooker with the cooking spray. Place the peaches and berries into the cooker.

2. Stir the juice, cornstarch and almond extract in a small bowl. Pour into the cooker.

3. Sprinkle the cake mix over the fruit mixture. Dot with the butter.

4. Layer **8** pieces of paper towel across the top of the cooker. Place the cooker cover on top.*

5. Cook on LOW for 4 to 5 hours** or until the fruit mixture boils and thickens and the topping is cooked through. Sprinkle with the confectioners' sugar.

*The paper towels will absorb any moisture that rises to the top of the cooker.

**Do not lift the cover on the cooker at all during the first 3 hours of the cook time.

Prep Time: 5 minutes
Cook Time: 4 hours
Total Time: 4 hours 5 minutes

Plum Cobbler with Cinnamon Drop Biscuits

MAKES 6 SERVINGS

6   cups sliced ripe plums
    (about 12 medium)

1   cup plus 2 tablespoons
    all-purpose flour, divided

8   tablespoons granulated sugar,
    divided

¼   cup packed brown sugar

1   tablespoon lemon juice

2   teaspoons baking powder

½   teaspoon ground cinnamon

¼   teaspoon salt

¼   cup (½ stick) cold butter,
    cut into pieces

8   to 10 tablespoons milk

1. Preheat oven to 400°F. Spray 8-inch square baking dish with nonstick cooking spray.

2. Combine plums, 2 tablespoons flour, 6 tablespoons granulated sugar, brown sugar and lemon juice in large bowl; toss to coat. Spoon into prepared baking dish. Bake 10 minutes.

3. Meanwhile, combine remaining 1 cup flour, 2 tablespoons granulated sugar, baking powder, cinnamon and salt in medium bowl. Cut in butter with pastry blender or two knives until mixture resembles coarse crumbs. Add milk, 1 tablespoon at a time, stirring until sticky dough forms. Drop heaping tablespoonfuls of dough onto plum mixture.

4. Bake 20 minutes or until golden brown. Serve warm.

Nectarine Raspberry Cobbler

MAKES 6 SERVINGS

3 cups sliced peeled nectarines or peaches (about 1¼ pounds)

½ cup fresh raspberries

3 tablespoons sugar, divided

1 tablespoon cornstarch

½ teaspoon ground cinnamon

¾ cup all-purpose flour

1 teaspoon grated lemon peel

¾ teaspoon baking powder

¼ teaspoon salt

⅛ teaspoon baking soda

3 tablespoons cold butter, cut into pieces

½ cup buttermilk

1. Preheat oven to 375°F. Combine nectarines and raspberries in large bowl.

2. Combine 2 tablespoons sugar, cornstarch and cinnamon in small bowl. Add to fruit; toss to coat. Spoon into 8-inch round baking dish.

3. Combine flour, lemon peel, baking powder, salt, baking soda and remaining 1 tablespoon sugar in medium bowl. Cut in butter with pastry blender or two knives until mixture resembles coarse crumbs. Stir in buttermilk until blended. Drop dough in six equal spoonfuls onto fruit.

4. Bake 25 to 27 minutes or until filling is bubbly and topping is just beginning to brown. Serve warm.

Note: One pound of frozen unsweetened peach slices and ½ cup frozen unsweetened raspberries may be substituted for the fresh fruit. Let the peach slices stand at room temperature until almost thawed, at least 2 hours. Use the raspberries frozen. Bake an additional 3 to 5 minutes or until the filling is bubbly and the topping is beginning to brown.

Cinnamon Roll-Topped Berry Cobbler

MAKES 8 SERVINGS

2 packages (12 ounces each) frozen mixed berries

1 cup sugar

¼ cup quick-cooking tapioca

¼ cup water

2 teaspoons vanilla

1 package (about 12 ounces) refrigerated cinnamon rolls with icing

Slow Cooker Directions

1. Combine frozen berries, sugar, tapioca, water and vanilla in slow cooker; stir until well blended. Top with cinnamon rolls.

2. Cover; cook on LOW 4 to 5 hours. Drizzle with icing; serve warm.

tip Make sure to use quick-cooking tapioca (also called instant tapioca), which is granulated, in this recipe. Regular tapioca consists of small pearls which don't fully dissolve when cooked.

Peach Cranberry Cobbler with Corn Bread Biscuits

MAKES 6 SERVINGS

1 package (16 ounces) frozen unsweetened sliced peaches, thawed

1 cup fresh or frozen cranberries or raspberries

⅓ cup orange juice

¼ cup packed brown sugar

2 tablespoons plus ⅓ cup all-purpose flour, divided

⅛ teaspoon ground allspice

3 tablespoons yellow cornmeal

1 tablespoon granulated sugar

1 teaspoon baking powder

¼ teaspoon salt

2 tablespoons cold butter, cut into pieces

1 egg

3 tablespoons milk

1. Preheat oven to 400°F. Combine peaches, cranberries and orange juice in large bowl.

2. Combine brown sugar, 2 tablespoons flour and allspice in small bowl. Add to peach mixture; toss to coat. Spoon into 8-inch square baking dish.

3. Combine remaining ⅓ cup flour, cornmeal, granulated sugar, baking powder and salt in medium bowl. Cut in butter with pastry blender or two knives until mixture resembles coarse crumbs. Whisk egg and milk in small bowl. Stir egg mixture into flour mixture with fork just until moistened. Spoon biscuit topping evenly over peach mixture.

4. Bake 30 to 35 minutes or until toothpick inserted into topping comes out clean.

Variation: Bake individual cobblers using six 8-ounce custard cups or ramekins. Bake 20 to 25 minutes or until toothpick inserted into topping comes out clean.

Berry Cobbler Cake

MAKES 6 SERVINGS

2 cups (1 pint) fresh or frozen berries (blueberries, blackberries and/or raspberries)

1 package (9 ounces) yellow cake mix

1 teaspoon ground cinnamon

1 egg

1 cup water, divided

¼ cup sugar

1 tablespoon cornstarch

Ice cream (optional)

1. Preheat oven to 375°F. Place berries in 9-inch square baking pan.

2. Combine cake mix and cinnamon in large bowl. Add egg and ¼ cup water; stir until well blended. Spoon over berries.

3. Combine sugar and cornstarch in small bowl. Stir in remaining ¾ cup water until sugar mixture dissolves; pour over cake batter and berries. (Do not stir.)

4. Bake 40 to 45 minutes or until golden brown. Serve warm or at room temperature with ice cream, if desired.

Crunch Peach Cobbler

MAKES ABOUT 6 TO 8 SERVINGS

⅓ cup plus 1 tablespoon granulated sugar, divided

1 tablespoon cornstarch

1 can (29 ounces) *or* 2 cans (16 ounces each) cling peach slices in juice, drained and ¾ cup juice reserved

½ teaspoon vanilla

2 cups all-purpose flour, divided

½ cup packed brown sugar

⅓ cup old-fashioned or quick oats

¼ cup (½ stick) butter, melted

½ teaspoon ground cinnamon

½ teaspoon salt

½ cup shortening, cut into pieces

4 to 5 tablespoons cold water

Whipped cream (optional)

1. Combine ⅓ cup granulated sugar and cornstarch in small saucepan. Slowly stir in reserved ¾ cup peach juice until well blended. Cook over low heat until thickened, stirring constantly. Stir in vanilla. Set aside.

2. Combine ½ cup flour, brown sugar, oats, butter and cinnamon in small bowl; stir until mixture resembles coarse crumbs.

3. Preheat oven to 350°F. Combine remaining 1½ cups flour, 1 tablespoon granulated sugar and salt in medium bowl. Cut in shortening with pastry blender or two knives until mixture resembles coarse crumbs. Sprinkle water, 1 tablespoon at a time, over flour mixture. Toss lightly with fork after each addition until mixture holds together. Press together to form a ball.

4. Roll out dough into 10-inch square, ⅛ inch thick. Place dough in 8-inch square baking dish; press onto bottom and about 1 inch up sides of dish. Arrange peaches in crust. Pour reserved peach sauce over peaches; sprinkle with crumb mixture.

5. Bake 45 minutes or until topping is golden brown. Serve warm or at room temperature with whipped cream, if desired.

Spicy Raisin, Date and Candied Ginger Cobbler

⅔ cup granulated sugar

2 tablespoons cornstarch

2 cups raisins

1 cup pitted dates, chopped

1 cup orange juice

⅓ cup water

2 tablespoons finely chopped candied ginger

3 tablespoons butter, divided

1 tablespoon lemon juice

½ teaspoon salt

1 small orange, peeled, quartered and thinly sliced

1 package (10 ounces) refrigerated biscuits

2 tablespoons packed brown sugar

Whipped cream (optional)

1. Preheat oven to 450°F. Combine granulated sugar and cornstarch in large saucepan. Stir in raisins, dates, orange juice, water and ginger; bring to a simmer over medium heat. Cook until liquid is slightly thickened, stirring constantly.

2. Remove from heat; stir in 1 tablespoon butter, lemon juice and salt. Fold in orange slices. Pour into 2-quart baking dish.

3. Split biscuits in half horizontally; arrange biscuit halves over raisin mixture. Melt remaining 2 tablespoons butter. Brush biscuits with butter; sprinkle with brown sugar.

4. Bake 10 minutes. *Reduce oven temperature to 350°F.* Bake 15 to 20 minutes or until biscuits are golden brown. Remove to wire rack. Serve warm or at room temperature with whipped cream, if desired.

Fresh Berry-Berry Cobbler

MAKES 6 SERVINGS

¼ cup sugar

1 teaspoon cornstarch

12 ounces fresh raspberries

8 ounces fresh blueberries

¼ cup CREAM OF WHEAT®
Hot Cereal (Instant, 1-minute,
2½-minute or 10-minute
cook time), uncooked

¼ cup all-purpose flour

¼ cup ground almonds

2 teaspoons baking powder

¼ teaspoon salt

¼ cup (½ stick) butter, cut into
small pieces, softened

¼ cup milk

1 egg

1 tablespoon sugar

Ice cream or whipped cream
(optional)

1. Preheat oven to 450°F. Blend sugar and cornstarch in mixing bowl. Add berries and toss to coat. Pour into 8-inch square baking pan; set aside.

2. Combine Cream of Wheat, flour, almonds, baking powder and salt in food processor. Add butter; pulse several times until well combined. Add milk and egg; pulse until mixed thoroughly. Spread evenly over fruit mixture. Sprinkle sugar over top.

3. Bake 20 minutes. Let stand 5 minutes before serving. Serve in shallow bowls with ice cream or whipped cream, if desired.

Prep Time: 10 minutes
Start to Finish Time: 35 minutes

tip For an elegant presentation, serve in a martini glass
and top with a fresh sprig of mint.

Tangy Cranberry Cobbler

MAKES 6 SERVINGS

2 cups thawed frozen or fresh cranberries

1 cup dried cranberries

1 cup raisins

½ cup orange juice

¼ cup plus 2 tablespoons sugar, divided

2 teaspoons cornstarch

1 cup all-purpose flour

2 teaspoons baking powder

1 teaspoon ground cinnamon

¼ teaspoon salt

¼ cup (½ stick) cold butter, cut into small pieces

½ cup milk

Whipped cream or vanilla ice cream (optional)

1. Preheat oven to 400°F. Combine cranberries, dried cranberries, raisins, orange juice, ¼ cup sugar and cornstarch in 9-inch square baking dish; toss to coat.

2. Combine flour, remaining 2 tablespoons sugar, baking powder, cinnamon and salt in large bowl. Cut in butter with pastry blender or two knives until mixture resembles coarse crumbs. Add milk; stir just until moistened. Drop batter by large spoonfuls onto cranberry mixture.

3. Bake 35 to 40 minutes or until topping is golden brown. Serve warm with whipped cream, if desired.

Berry Peachy Cobbler

MAKES 8 SERVINGS

4 tablespoons plus 2 teaspoons sugar, divided

¾ cup plus 2 tablespoons all-purpose flour, divided

1¼ pounds peaches, peeled and sliced *or* 1 package (16 ounces) frozen unsweetened sliced peaches, thawed and drained

2 cups fresh raspberries *or* 1 package (12 ounces) frozen unsweetened raspberries

1 teaspoon grated lemon peel

½ teaspoon baking powder

½ teaspoon baking soda

⅛ teaspoon salt

2 tablespoons cold butter, cut into small pieces

½ cup buttermilk

1. Preheat oven to 425°F. Spray eight ramekins or 11×7-inch baking dish with nonstick cooking spray. Place ramekins in baking dish.

2. Combine 2 tablespoons sugar and 2 tablespoons flour in large bowl. Add peaches, raspberries and lemon peel; toss to coat. Divide fruit evenly among prepared ramekins.

3. Bake 15 minutes or until fruit is bubbly around edges. Meanwhile, combine remaining ¾ cup flour, 2 tablespoons sugar, baking powder, baking soda and salt in medium bowl. Cut in butter with pastry blender or two knives until mixture resembles coarse crumbs. Stir in buttermilk just until dry ingredients are moistened.

4. Remove ramekins from oven; top fruit with dollops of topping. Sprinkle topping with remaining 2 teaspoons sugar. Bake 18 to 20 minutes or until topping is lightly browned. Serve warm.

Slow Cooker Mixed Berry Cobbler

MAKES 8 SERVINGS

1 package (16 ounces) frozen mixed berries

¾ cup granulated sugar

2 tablespoons quick-cooking tapioca

2 teaspoons grated lemon peel

1½ cups all-purpose flour

½ cup packed brown sugar

2¼ teaspoons baking powder

¼ teaspoon ground nutmeg

¾ cup milk

⅓ cup butter, melted

Ice cream (optional)

Slow Cooker Directions

1. Combine berries, granulated sugar, tapioca and lemon peel in slow cooker; toss to coat.

2. Combine flour, brown sugar, baking powder and nutmeg in medium bowl. Add milk and butter; stir just until blended. Drop spoonfuls of dough onto berry mixture.

3. Cover; cook on LOW 4 hours. Uncover; let stand about 30 minutes. Serve warm with ice cream, if desired.

Easy Peach Cobbler

MAKES 6 SERVINGS

8 cups peeled and sliced peaches, nectarines or apples (½-inch-thick slices)

1 cup granulated sugar

⅔ cup plus 2 tablespoons BISQUICK®, divided

1 teaspoon ground cinnamon

2 tablespoons firmly packed brown sugar

¼ cup (½ stick) I CAN'T BELIEVE IT'S NOT BUTTER!® Spread

2 tablespoons milk

Preheat oven to 400°F.

In large bowl, combine peaches, granulated sugar, 2 tablespoons baking mix and cinnamon. In 11×7-inch baking dish, arrange peach mixture; set aside.

In medium bowl, mix remaining ⅔ cup baking mix with brown sugar. With pastry blender or 2 knives, cut in I Can't Believe It's Not Butter!® Spread until mixture is size of small peas. Stir in milk just until moistened. Drop by teaspoonfuls onto peach mixture.

Bake 30 minutes or until peaches are tender and topping is golden. Let stand 5 minutes before serving. Serve warm with vanilla ice cream, if desired.

Prep Time: 15 minutes
Cook Time: 30 minutes

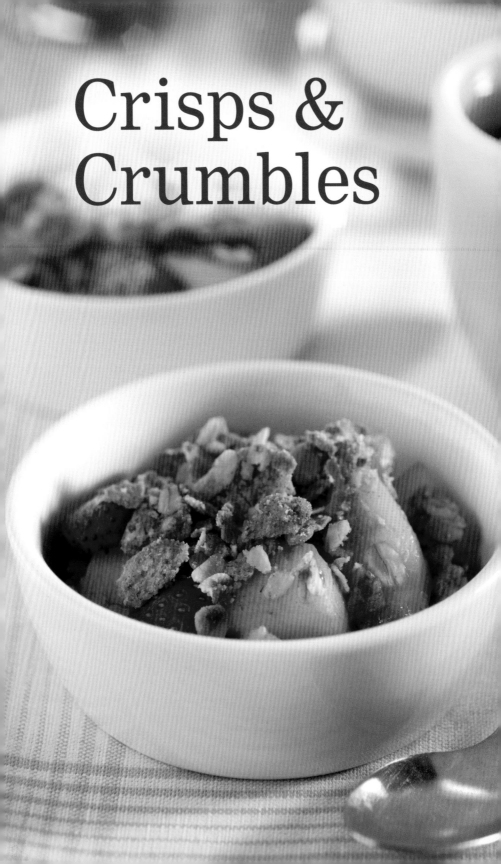

Crisps & Crumbles

Strawberry and Peach Crisp

MAKES 4 SERVINGS

1 cup frozen peach slices, thawed and cut into 1-inch pieces

1 cup sliced fresh strawberries

3 teaspoons sugar, divided

¼ cup bran cereal flakes

2 tablespoons old-fashioned oats

1 tablespoon all-purpose flour

⅛ teaspoon ground cinnamon

⅛ teaspoon salt

1 tablespoon butter, cut into pieces

1. Preheat oven to 325°F. Spray 1- to 1½-quart baking dish with nonstick cooking spray.

2. Combine peaches and strawberries in medium bowl. Sprinkle with 1 teaspoon sugar; toss to coat. Spoon into prepared baking dish.

3. Combine cereal, oats, flour, cinnamon and salt in medium bowl. Stir in remaining 2 teaspoons sugar. Add butter; stir with fork until mixture resembles coarse crumbs. Sprinkle over fruit in baking dish.

4. Bake 20 minutes or until filling is bubbly and topping is lightly browned.

Variation: For a strawberry crisp, omit the peaches and use 2 cups strawberries in the recipe.

Plum Rhubarb Crumble

MAKES 6 TO 8 SERVINGS

1½ pounds plums, each pitted and cut into 8 wedges (4 cups)

1½ pounds rhubarb, cut into ½-inch pieces (5 cups)

1 cup granulated sugar

1 teaspoon finely grated fresh ginger

¼ teaspoon ground nutmeg

3 tablespoons cornstarch

¾ cup old-fashioned oats

½ cup all-purpose flour

½ cup packed brown sugar

½ cup sliced almonds, toasted*

¼ teaspoon salt

½ cup (1 stick) cold butter, cut into pieces

To toast almonds, spread in single layer on ungreased baking sheet. Bake in preheated 350°F oven 5 minutes or until golden brown, stirring frequently.

1. Combine plums, rhubarb, granulated sugar, ginger and nutmeg in large bowl; toss to coat. Cover and let stand at room temperature 2 hours.

2. Preheat oven to 375°F. Spray 9-inch round or square baking dish with nonstick cooking spray. Line baking sheet with foil.

3. Pour juices from fruit into small saucepan; bring to a boil over medium-high heat. Cook about 12 minutes or until reduced to syrupy consistency, stirring occasionally. Stir in cornstarch until well blended. Stir mixture into bowl with fruit; pour into prepared baking dish.

4. Combine oats, flour, brown sugar, almonds and salt in medium bowl. Add butter; mix with fingertips until butter is evenly distributed and mixture is clumpy. Sprinkle evenly over fruit. Place dish on prepared baking sheet.

5. Bake about 50 minutes or until filling is bubbly and topping is golden brown. Cool 1 hour before serving.

Mango Raspberry Crisp

MAKES 4 SERVINGS

1 mango, peeled, seeded and chopped into ½-inch pieces

1 cup fresh raspberries

½ cup old-fashioned oats

2 tablespoons packed brown sugar

½ to 1 teaspoon ground cinnamon

2 tablespons butter, cut into pieces

2 tablespoons chopped pecans

1. Preheat oven to 400°F. Spray four 6-ounce custard cups or ramekins with nonstick cooking spray.

2. Divide mango and raspberries evenly among custard cups.

3. Combine oats, brown sugar and cinnamon in medium bowl. Cut in butter with pastry blender or two knives until mixture resembles coarse crumbs. Stir in pecans. Sprinkle evenly over fruit.

4. Bake 20 to 25 minutes or until fruit is tender and topping is golden brown. Let stand 15 minutes before serving.

Apple Blackberry Crisp

4   cups sliced peeled apples

Juice of ½ lemon

2   tablespoons granulated sugar

2   tablespoons Irish cream liqueur

1   teaspoon ground cinnamon, divided

1   cup old-fashioned oats

6   tablespoons (¾ stick) cold butter, cut into pieces

⅔   cup packed brown sugar

¼   cup all-purpose flour

1   cup fresh blackberries

Whipped cream or ice cream (optional)

1. Preheat oven to 375°F. Grease 9-inch oval or 8-inch square baking dish.

2. Place apples in large bowl; drizzle with lemon juice. Add granulated sugar, liqueur and ½ teaspoon cinnamon; toss to coat.

3. Combine oats, butter, brown sugar, flour and remaining ½ teaspoon cinnamon in food processor; pulse unti combined, leaving some some chunks remaining.

4. Gently stir blackberries into apple mixture. Spoon into prepared baking dish; sprinkle with oat mixture.

5. Bake 30 to 40 minutes or until filling is bubbly and topping is golden brown. Serve warm with whipped cream, if desired.

tip This crisp can also be made without the blackberries; just add an additional 1 cup sliced apples.

Quick Peach Crisp

MAKES 5 SERVINGS

4 cups sliced peeled peaches or nectarines (about 4 large peaches or nectarines)

3 tablespoons cinnamon-sugar (see Tip)

12 to 14 pecan shortbread cookies,* coarsely chopped

Or substitute 20 vanilla wafers.

Slow Cooker Directions

1. Preheat oven to 350°F. Place peaches in 9-inch square baking dish.

2. Add cinnamon-sugar; toss to coat. Sprinkle with cookies.

3. Bake 25 to 30 minutes or until peaches are tender and cookies are lightly browned.

tip Cinnamon-sugar is available in most large supermarkets. Look for it in the spice or baking section. However, you can easily make your own by mixing together 1 cup sugar and 1 tablespoon ground cinnamon. Store cinnamon-sugar in a glass jar. Sprinkle it on buttered toast or applesauce.

Strawberry Rhubarb Crisp

MAKES 8 SERVINGS

4 cups sliced rhubarb
(1-inch pieces)

3 cups sliced strawberries
(about 1 pint)

¾ cup granulated sugar

⅓ cup plus ¼ cup all-purpose
flour, divided

1 tablespoon grated lemon peel

1 cup quick oats

½ cup packed brown sugar

1 teaspoon ground cinnamon

½ teaspoon salt

⅓ cup butter, melted

1. Preheat oven to 375°F. Combine rhubarb and strawberries in large bowl.

2. Combine granulated sugar, ¼ cup flour and lemon peel in small bowl. Sprinkle over fruit; toss to coat. Spoon into 9-inch square baking pan.

3. Combine oats, brown sugar, remaining ⅓ cup flour, cinnamon and salt in medium bowl. Stir in butter until mixture is crumbly. Sprinkle over fruit mixture.

4. Bake 45 to 50 minutes or until filling is bubbly and topping is lightly browned. Serve warm or at room temperature.

Apple Cranberry Crumble

MAKES 4 SERVINGS

4 large apples (about 1⅓ pounds), peeled and cut into ¼-inch slices

2 cups fresh or frozen cranberries

⅓ cup granulated sugar

6 tablespoons all-purpose flour, divided

1 teaspoon apple pie spice, divided

¼ teaspoon salt, divided

½ cup chopped walnuts

¼ cup old-fashioned oats

2 tablespoons packed brown sugar

¼ cup (½ stick) butter, cut into pieces

1. Preheat oven to 375°F.

2. Combine apples, cranberries, granulated sugar, 2 tablespoons flour, ½ teaspoon apple pie spice and ⅛ teaspoon salt in large bowl; toss to coat. Spoon into medium (8-inch) cast iron skillet.

3. Combine remaining 4 tablespoons flour, walnuts, oats, brown sugar, remaining ½ teaspoon apple pie spice and ⅛ teaspoon salt in medium bowl; mix well. Cut in butter with pastry blender or two knives until mixture resembles coarse crumbs. Sprinkle evenly over fruit mixture.

4. Bake 50 to 60 minutes or until filling is bubbly and topping is lightly browned.

Peach and Blueberry Crisp

MAKES 4 SERVINGS

3 cups fresh or thawed frozen peach slices, undrained

1 cup fresh or thawed frozen blueberries, undrained

2 tablespoons granulated sugar

¼ teaspoon ground nutmeg

2 tablespoons old-fashioned oats

2 tablespoons crisp rice cereal

2 tablespoons all-purpose flour

1 tablespoon packed brown sugar

1 tablespoon butter, melted

⅛ teaspoon ground cinnamon

1. Preheat oven to 375°F. Combine peaches and blueberries in ungreased 8-inch round cake pan.

2. Combine granulated sugar and nutmeg in small bowl. Sprinkle over fruit; toss gently to coat.

3. Combine oats, cereal, flour, brown sugar, butter and cinnamon in small bowl. Sprinkle over fruit mixture.

4. Bake 35 to 40 minutes or until peaches are tender and topping is golden brown.

tip Crisp recipes are very versatile and easy to change—simply swap out the fruit for what you prefer or what you have on hand. Try nectarines or plums instead of peaches, or use raspberries or halved strawberries instead of blueberries.

Best Ever Apple Crisp

MAKES 8 SERVINGS

8 cups thinly sliced peeled tart apples

1 cup packed brown sugar, divided

1 tablespoon cornstarch

1½ teaspoons ground cinnamon, divided

¼ cup all-purpose flour

¼ cup (½ stick) cold butter, cut into pieces

¾ cup old-fashioned oats

½ cup coarsely chopped pecans

Vanilla ice cream (optional)

1. Preheat oven to 350°F.

2. Combine apples, ½ cup brown sugar, cornstarch and 1 teaspoon cinnamon in large bowl; toss to coat. Spoon into 2-quart casserole.

3. Combine remaining ½ cup brown sugar, flour and remaining ½ teaspoon cinnamon in medium bowl; mix well. Cut in butter with pastry blender or two knives until mixture resembles coarse crumbs. Stir in oats and pecans. Sprinkle evenly over apple mixture.

4. Bake 40 to 45 minutes or until apples are tender and topping is golden brown. Serve warm with ice cream, if desired.

Double Cherry Crumbles

MAKES 8 SERVINGS

½ (16-ounce) package refrigerated oatmeal raisin cookie dough*

½ cup old-fashioned oats

¾ teaspoon ground cinnamon

½ teaspoon ground ginger

2 tablespoons cold butter, cut into pieces

1 cup chopped pecans, toasted**

2 cans (21 ounces each) cherry pie filling

1 package (16 ounces) frozen pitted unsweetened dark sweet cherries, thawed

*Save remaining ½ package of dough for another use.

**To toast pecans, spread in single layer on baking sheet. Bake in preheated 350°F oven 5 to 7 minutes or until golden brown, stirring frequently.

1. Let dough stand at room temperature 15 minutes. Spray eight 4-ounce ramekins with nonstick cooking spray; place on rimmed baking sheet.

2. Preheat oven to 350°F. Beat dough, oats, cinnamon and ginger in large bowl until well blended. Cut in butter with pastry blender or two knives. Stir in pecans.

3. Combine pie filling and cherries in large bowl. Divide cherry mixture evenly among prepared ramekins; sprinkle with pecan mixture.

4. Bake 25 minutes or until topping is golden brown. Serve warm.

Slow Cooker Five-Spice Apple Crisp >

MAKES 4 SERVINGS

3 tablespoons butter, melted

6 Golden Delicious apples, peeled and cut into ½-inch-thick slices

2 teaspoons lemon juice

¼ cup packed brown sugar

¾ teaspoon Chinese five-spice powder

1 cup coarsely crushed Chinese-style almond cookies or almond biscotti

Whipped cream (optional)

Slow Cooker Directions

1. Brush inside of slow cooker with melted butter. Add apples and lemon juice; toss to coat. Sprinkle with brown sugar and five-spice powder; toss to coat.

2. Cover; cook on LOW 3½ hours or until apples are tender. Sprinkle cookies over apples. Serve warm with whipped cream, if desired.

Autumn Fruit Crisp

MAKES 6 SERVINGS

⅓ cup old-fashioned oats

¼ cup packed brown sugar

2 tablespoons whole wheat flour

½ teaspoon ground cinnamon

2 tablespoons cold butter, cut into small pieces

2 baking apples, peeled and sliced (1 pound)

1 pear, peeled and sliced (8 ounces)

1. Preheat oven to 350°F. Spray 8-inch square baking dish with nonstick cooking spray.

2. Combine oats, brown sugar, flour and cinnamon in medium bowl; mix well. Cut in butter with pastry blender or two knives until mixture resembles coarse crumbs.

3. Combine apples and pears in baking dish; sprinkle with oat mixture.

4. Bake 35 to 40 minutes or until fruit is tender and topping is lightly browned.

Triple Berry Fruit Crisp

MAKES 8 SERVINGS

1 bag (16 ounces) frozen mixed berry blend or 1⅓ cups each of blueberries, raspberries and strawberries)

¼ cup granulated sugar

1 tablespoon ARGO® Corn Starch

½ cup water

1 tablespoon lemon juice

½ teaspoon SPICE ISLANDS® Pure Almond Extract

½ cup (1 stick) butter or margarine, softened

1 cup packed brown sugar

1 cup quick oats (not instant)

⅓ cup all-purpose flour

½ teaspoon SPICE ISLANDS® Ground Saigon Cinnamon

1. Mix berries, granulated sugar and corn starch in a large bowl. Add water, lemon juice and almond extract. Pour mixture into a greased 8-inch square baking dish.

2. Combine butter, brown sugar, quick oats, flour and cinnamon in a bowl with a pastry blender until butter is in small pieces. Sprinkle over top of berries.

3. Bake in a preheated 350°F oven for 45 minutes until fruit is bubbly and topping is browned. Serve warm or at room temperature.

Serving Suggestion: Delicious with a scoop of vanilla ice cream.

Prep Time: 15 minutes
Bake Time: 45 minutes

Cinnamon Pear Crisp

MAKES 8 SERVINGS

8 pears, peeled and sliced

¾ cup unsweetened apple juice concentrate

½ cup golden raisins

¼ cup plus 3 tablespoons all-purpose flour, divided

1 teaspoon ground cinnamon

⅓ cup quick oats

3 tablespoons packed dark brown sugar

3 tablespoons butter, melted

1. Preheat oven to 375°F. Spray 11×7-inch baking dish with nonstick cooking spray.

2. Combine pears, apple juice concentrate, raisins, 3 tablespoons flour and cinnamon in large bowl; toss to coat. Spoon into prepared baking dish.

3. Combine oats, remaining ¼ cup flour, brown sugar and butter in medium bowl; stir until mixture resembles coarse crumbs. Sprinkle evenly over pear mixture.

4. Bake 1 hour or until topping is golden brown.

Cranberry Apple Crisp

MAKES 8 SERVINGS

Filling

- ½ cup granulated sugar
- 3 tablespoons ARGO® Corn Starch
- 1 teaspoon SPICE ISLANDS® Ground Saigon Cinnamon
- ½ teaspoon SPICE ISLANDS® Ground Nutmeg
- 5 to 6 cups peeled, cubed tart apples
- 1 cup fresh or frozen cranberries
- ½ cup KARO® Light Corn Syrup
- 1 teaspoon grated orange peel

Topping

- ½ cup walnuts or quick oats (not instant)
- ⅓ cup packed brown sugar
- ¼ cup all-purpose flour
- ¼ cup (½ stick) butter or margarine

1. Mlix granulated sugar, corn starch, cinnamon and nutmeg in a large bowl. Add apples, cranberries, corn syrup and orange peel; toss to combine. Spoon into shallow 2-quart baking dish.

2. Combine walnuts, brown sugar and flour in a small bowl. With a pastry blender or 2 knives, cut in butter until crumbly.

3. Top apple filling with walnut mixture.

4. Bake at 350°F for 50 minutes or until cranberries and apples are tender and juices that bubble up in center are shiny and clear. Cool slightly; serve warm.

Prep Time: 25 minutes
Cook Time: 50 minutes

Peach Ginger Crumble

MAKES 6 SERVINGS

1 package (16 ounces) frozen sliced peaches, thawed

2 ripe pears, sliced

¾ cup dried apricots, cut into ¼-inch pieces

4 tablespoons packed dark brown sugar, divided

1 tablespoon cornstarch

1 teaspoon vanilla

12 gingersnaps, finely crushed

1 tablespoon canola oil

½ teaspoon ground cinnamon

Whipped cream (optional)

1. Preheat oven to 350°F. Spray 9-inch deep-dish pie plate with nonstick cooking spray.

2. Combine peaches, pears, apricots, 2 tablespoons brown sugar, cornstarch and vanilla in large bowl; toss to coat. Spoon into prepared pie plate.

3. Combine crushed gingersnaps, remaining 2 tablespoons brown sugar, oil and cinnamon in small bowl. Sprinkle evenly over fruit mixture.

4. Bake 30 minutes or until filling is bubbly. Cool in pan on wire rack 10 minutes. Serve warm with whipped cream, if desired.

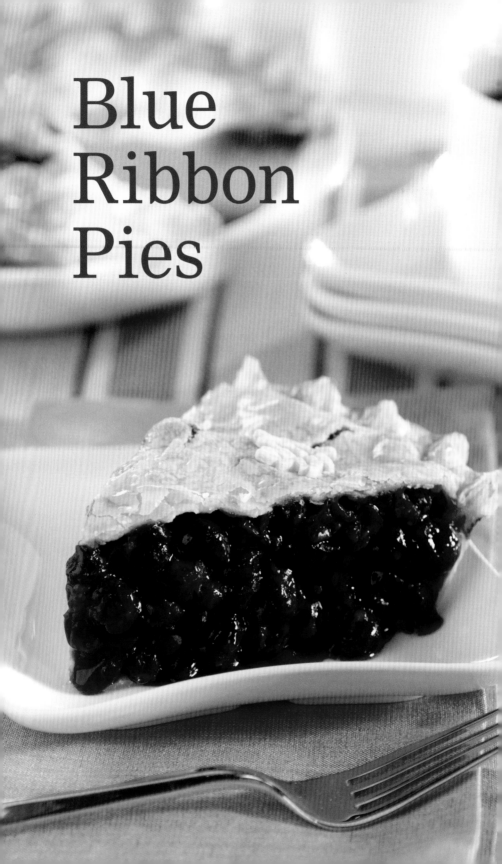

Blue
Ribbon
Pies

Blueberry Pie

MAKES 8 SERVINGS

Cream Cheese Pastry
(recipe follows)

4 cups fresh or thawed frozen
blueberries

2 tablespoons cornstarch

⅔ cup blueberry preserves, melted

¼ teaspoon ground nutmeg

1 egg yolk

1 tablespoon sour cream

1. Prepare Cream Cheese Pastry.

2. Preheat oven to 425°F. Roll out one pastry disc into 11-inch circle on floured surface. Line 9-inch pie plate with pastry.

3. Combine blueberries and cornstarch in medium bowl; toss gently to coat. Add preserves and nutmeg; mix gently. Spoon into crust.

4. Roll out remaining pastry disc into 11-inch circle; place over fruit mixture. Turn edge under; seal and flute edge. Cut several slits in top crust. If desired, cut leaves from pastry scraps to decorate top of pie.

5. Bake 10 minutes. *Reduce oven temperature to 350°F.* Combine egg yolk and sour cream in small bowl; brush lightly over crust. Bake 40 minutes or until crust is golden brown. Remove to wire rack to cool 15 minutes. Serve warm or at room temperature.

Cream Cheese Pastry: Combine 1½ cups all-purpose flour and ⅛ teaspoon salt in large bowl. Cut in ½ cup (1 stick) cold cubed butter with pastry blender or two knives until mixture resembles coarse crumbs. Cut in 3 ounces cold cubed cream cheese and 1 teaspoon vanilla until mixture forms dough. Divide dough in half. Shape each half into a disc; wrap with plastic wrap. Refrigerate 30 minutes.

Rhubarb and Sweet Cherry Pie

MAKES 8 SERVINGS

Double Crust Pie Pastry (recipe follows)

4 cups sliced (½-inch slices) fresh rhubarb (about 1¼ pounds)

1½ cups fresh or frozen Bing cherries, pitted and halved

1 cup sugar

2 tablespoons cornstarch

½ teaspoon ground cinnamon

⅛ teaspoon salt

2 tablespoons butter, cut into pieces

1. Prepare Double Crust Pie Pastry.

2. Preheat oven to 400°F. Combine rhubarb and cherries in large bowl. Combine sugar, cornstarch, cinnamon and salt in small bowl until blended. Add to rhubarb mixture; toss to coat.

3. Roll out one pastry disc into 12-inch circle on floured surface. Line 9-inch pie plate with pastry, allowing excess to hang over edge.

4. Roll out remaining pastry disc into 11-inch circle. Cut into ¾-inch-wide strips with sharp knife.

5. Spoon fruit mixture into crust; dot with butter. Arrange pastry strips in lattice design over fruit. Tuck ends of strips under edge of bottom crust; seal and flute edge.

6. Bake about 45 minutes or until rhubarb is tender and filling is bubbly, covering pie loosely with foil during last 10 minutes to prevent overbrowning. Cool on wire rack. Serve warm or at room temperature.

Double Crust Pie Pastry: Combine 2 cups all-purpose flour and 1 teaspoon salt in large bowl. Cut in 6 tablespoons cold cubed shortening and 4 tablespoons (½ stick) cold cubed butter with pastry blender or two knives until mixture resembles coarse crumbs. Combine 4 tablespoons ice water and ½ teaspoon cider vinegar in small bowl. Add to flour mixture; mix with fork until dough forms, adding additional water as needed. Divide dough in half. Shape each half into a disc; wrap with plastic wrap. Refrigerate 1 hour.

Tip: Frozen sliced rhubarb can be substituted for fresh. Bake at 400°F for 50 to 55 minutes or until the rhubarb is tender and the filling is bubbly, covering loosely with foil during the last 15 minutes of baking to prevent overbrowning.

Cranberry Apple Nut Pie

MAKES 8 SERVINGS

Rich Pie Pastry (recipe follows)

1 cup sugar

3 tablespoons all-purpose flour

¼ teaspoon salt

4 cups sliced peeled tart apples (4 large apples)

2 cups fresh cranberries

½ cup golden raisins

½ cup coarsely chopped pecans

1 tablespoon grated lemon peel

2 tablespoons butter, cut into pieces

1 egg, beaten

1. Prepare Rich Pie Pastry.

2. Preheat oven to 425°F. Roll out one pastry disc into 11-inch circle on floured surface. Line 9-inch pie plate with pastry.

3. Combine sugar, flour and salt in large bowl. Stir in apples, cranberries, raisins, pecans and lemon peel; toss to coat. Spoon into crust; dot with butter.

4. Roll remaining pastry disc into 11-inch circle. Place over fruit mixture. Trim, seal and flute edge. Cut three slits in center of top crust. Lightly brush pastry with egg.

5. Bake 35 minutes or until apples are tender and crust is golden brown. Cool 15 minutes on wire rack. Serve warm or cool completely.

Rich Pie Pastry: Combine 2 cups all-purpose flour and ¼ teaspoon salt in large bowl. Cut in 6 tablespoons (¾ stick) cold cubed butter and 6 tablespoons cold cubed shortening with pastry blender or two knives until mixture resembles coarse crumbs. Sprinkle with 6 to 8 tablespoons cold water, 1 tablespoon at a time, stirring just until dough comes together. Divide dough in half. Shape each half into a disc; wrap with plastic wrap. Refrigerate 30 minutes.

Peach Raspberry Pie

MAKES 7 TO 8 SERVINGS

Single Crust Pie Pastry
(recipe follows)

Almond Crumb Topping
(recipe follows)

5 cups sliced peeled peaches
(about 2 pounds)

2 tablespoons lemon juice

1 cup fresh raspberries

½ cup sugar

2 tablespoons quick-cooking
tapioca

½ teaspoon ground cinnamon

¼ teaspoon ground nutmeg

Whipped cream (optional)

1. Prepare Single-Crust Pie Pastry and Almond Crumb Topping.

2. Preheat oven to 400°F. Roll out pastry into 11-inch circle on floured surface.
Line 9-inch pie plate with pastry; flute edge. Refrigerate 15 minutes.

3. Place peaches in large bowl. Sprinkle with lemon juice; toss to coat. Gently stir
in raspberries.

4. Combine sugar, tapioca, cinnamon and nutmeg in small bowl. Sprinkle over fruit
mixture; toss to coat. Spoon into crust; sprinkle with Almond Crumb Topping.

5. Bake 15 minutes. *Reduce oven temperature to 350°F.* Bake 30 minutes or until
filling is bubbly. Cool 15 minutes on wire rack. Serve warm or at room temperature
with whipped cream, if desired.

Single Crust Pie Pastry: Combine 1¼ cups all-purpose flour and ½ teaspoon
salt in large bowl. Cut in 3 tablespoons cold cubed shortening and 3 tablespoons
cold cubed butter with pastry blender or two knives until mixture resembles coarse
crumbs. Combine 3 tablespoons ice water and ½ teaspoon cider vinegar in small
bowl. Add to flour mixture; mix with fork until dough forms, adding additional
water as needed. Shape dough into a disc; wrap with plastic wrap. Refrigerate
30 minutes.

Almond Crumb Topping: Combine ⅔ cup old-fashioned or quick oats, ¼ cup
all-purpose flour, ¼ cup packed brown sugar, ¼ cup slivered almonds and
½ teaspoon ground cinnamon in medium bowl. Stir in 3 tablespoons softened
butter until mixture resembles coarse crumbs.

Tip: To substitute frozen fruit, thaw 5 cups frozen sliced peaches in large bowl
1½ to 2 hours. Continue with step 3, using frozen raspberries (do not thaw).
Bake as directed in step 5.

Lattice-Topped Cherry Pie

MAKES 1 PIE

Pie Pastry (recipe follows)

6 cups pitted sweet Bing cherries

¾ cup plus 1 teaspoon sugar, divided

3 tablespoons plus 1 teaspoon cornstarch

2 tablespoons lemon juice

Half-and-half

1. Prepare Pie Pastry.

2. Preheat oven to 400°F. Combine cherries, ¾ cup sugar, cornstarch and lemon juice in large bowl; toss to coat. Let stand 15 minutes or until syrup forms.

3. Roll out one pastry disc into 12-circle (about ⅛ inch thick) on floured surface. Line 9-inch pie plate with pastry, allowing excess to drape over edge.

4. Roll out remaining pastry disc into 11-inch circle. Cut into ½-inch-wide strips with sharp knife.

5. Spoon cherry mixture into crust. Arrange pastry strips in lattice design over fruit. Tuck ends of strips under edge of bottom crust; seal edge. Brush pastry with half-and-half; sprinkle with remaining 1 teaspoon sugar. Cover loosely with foil.

6. Bake 30 minutes. Remove foil; bake 30 minutes or until filling is thick and bubbly and crust is golden brown. Cool on wire rack.

Pie Pastry: Combine 2¼ cups all-purpose flour and ¾ teaspoon salt in large bowl. Cut in ½ cup cold cubed shortening and 2 tablespoons cold cubed butter with pastry blender or two knives until mixture resembles coarse crumbs. Drizzle with 5 to 6 tablespoons cold water, 1 tablespoon at a time, stirring just until dough comes together. Divide dough in half. Shape each half into a disc; wrap with plastic wrap. Refrigerate 30 minutes.

Plum and Walnut Pie

MAKES 8 SERVINGS

Single Crust Pie Pastry (recipe follows)

Oat Streusel (recipe follows)

8 cups thinly sliced plums

⅓ cup granulated sugar

⅓ cup packed brown sugar

3 to 4 tablespoons all-purpose flour

1 tablespoon honey

½ teaspoon ground cinnamon

¼ teaspoon ground ginger

⅛ teaspoon salt

½ cup candied walnuts

1. Prepare Single Crust Pie Pastry and Oat Streusel.

2. Preheat oven to 425°F. Place plums in large bowl. Add granulated sugar, brown sugar, 3 tablespoons flour (use 4 tablespoons if plums are very juicy), honey, cinnamon, ginger and salt; toss to coat.

3. Roll out pastry into 11-inch circle on floured surface. Line 9-inch pie pan with pastry; flute edge. Spoon plum mixture into crust; sprinkle with Oat Streusel. Place pie on baking sheet.

4. Bake 15 minutes. *Reduce oven temperature to 350°F.* Sprinkle pie with walnuts. Bake 30 minutes. Lightly tent pie with foil. Bake 30 minutes or until filling is bubbly and crust is golden brown. Cool at least 30 minutes before slicing.

Single Crust Pie Pastry: Combine 1¼ cups all-purpose flour and ½ teaspoon salt in large bowl. Cut in 3 tablespoons cold cubed shortening and 3 tablespoons cold cubed butter with pastry blender or two knives until mixture resembles coarse crumbs. Combine 3 tablespoons ice water and ½ teaspoon cider vinegar in small bowl. Add to flour mixture; mix with fork until dough forms, adding additional water as needed. Shape dough into a disc; wrap with plastic wrap. Refrigerate 30 minutes.

Oat Streusel: Combine ¼ cup all-purpose flour, ¼ cup old-fashioned oats, ¼ cup granulated sugar, ¼ cup packed brown sugar and ⅛ teaspoon salt in medium bowl. Add ¼ cup (½ stick) cubed butter; crumble with fingertips until mixture resembles coarse crumbs.

Note: Candied walnuts are sold in packages in the baking section of the supermarket; they may also be found in the produce section where salad ingredients are sold.

Dole® Very Peachy Pie

MAKES 1 (9-INCH) PIE

¾ cup sugar

3½ tablespoons minute tapioca

¼ teaspoon salt

6 cups DOLE® Frozen Sliced Peaches, thawed

1 tablespoon lemon juice

¼ teaspoon grated lemon peel

Pastry for 9-inch double-crust pie

2 tablespoons butter or margarine, cut into small pieces

Milk

COMBINE sugar, tapioca and salt in small bowl.

COMBINE peaches, lemon juice, lemon peel and sugar mixture in large bowl; mix well.

ROLL out half of pastry and fit into pie pan. Roll out remaining pastry.

SPOON peach mixture into pie pan. Dot with butter. Top with remaining pastry; trim, turn under and flute edges.

CUT a few slits in top. Brush lightly with milk and sprinkle with additional sugar, if desired.

LIGHTLY cover edges with thin strips of aluminum foil. Bake at 425°F 20 minutes. Remove foil and bake 20 to 25 minutes longer or until golden brown. Cool on wire rack.

Prep Time: 20 minutes
Bake Time: 45 minutes

Apple Pie with Cheddar

MAKES 8 SERVINGS

Single Crust Pie Pastry
(recipe follows)

Streusel (recipe follows)

8 cups sliced peeled apples (Rome Beauty, Fuji or Northern Spy)

½ cup packed dark brown sugar

⅓ cup granulated sugar

3 tablespoons all-purpose flour

½ teaspoon ground cinnamon

¼ teaspoon salt

1 cup (4 ounces) shredded sharp Cheddar cheese, divided

1. Prepare Single Crust Pie Pastry and Streusel.

2. Preheat oven to 425°F. Place apples in large bowl. Add brown sugar, granulated sugar, flour, cinnamon and salt; toss to coat.

3. Roll out pastry into 11-inch circle on floured surface. Sprinkle with ½ cup cheese; roll lightly to adhere. Line 9-inch pie plate with pastry; flute edge.

4. Spoon filling into crust, packing down. Sprinkle with Streusel. Place pie on baking sheet.

5. Bake 15 minutes. *Reduce oven temperature to 350°F.* Lightly tent pie with foil; bake 35 minutes. Remove foil; sprinkle with remaining ½ cup cheese. Bake 10 minutes or until cheese is melted and crust is golden brown. Cool at least 30 minutes before slicing.

Single Crust Pie Pastry: Combine 1¼ cups all-purpose flour and ½ teaspoon salt in large bowl. Cut in 3 tablespoons cold cubed shortening and 3 tablespoons cold cubed butter with pastry blender or two knives until mixture resembles coarse crumbs. Combine 3 tablespoons ice water and ½ teaspoon cider vinegar in small bowl. Add to flour mixture; mix with fork until dough forms, adding additional water as needed. Shape dough into a disc; wrap with plastic wrap. Refrigerate 30 minutes.

Streusel: Combine ⅓ cup all-purpose flour, ⅓ cup granulated sugar, ⅓ cup packed dark brown sugar and ¼ teaspoon salt in medium bowl. Cut in 5 tablespoons cubed butter with pastry blender or two knives until mixture resembles coarse crumbs.

Blackberry Custard Pie

MAKES 8 SERVINGS

Pie Pastry (recipe follows)

½ cup sugar

3 tablespoons cornstarch

1¼ cups milk

2 teaspoons grated lemon peel

1 tablespoon lemon juice

2 eggs, lightly beaten

1 pint fresh blackberries

1. Prepare Pie Pastry.

2. Preheat oven to 425°F. Flatten pastry to 1-inch thickness on 12-inch square of waxed paper; cover with second square of waxed paper. Roll out gently into 12-inch circle. Mend any tears or ragged edges by pressing together with fingers. *Do not moisten.* Remove top layer of waxed paper. Place pastry, waxed paper side up, in 9-inch pie plate; carefully peel off paper. Press pastry gently into pie plate and flute edge. Pierce crust with fork at ¼-inch intervals, about 40 times. Cut square of foil about 4 inches larger than pie plate. Line crust with foil; fill with dried beans, uncooked rice or ceramic pie weights.

3. Bake 10 minutes or until set. Remove foil lining and beans. Bake 5 minutes or until crust is lightly browned. Cool completely on wire rack.

4. Combine sugar and cornstarch in small saucepan. Stir in milk, lemon peel and lemon juice; cook and stir over medium heat until mixture boils and thickens. Boil 1 minute, stirring constantly. Stir about ½ cup hot milk mixture into eggs; stir egg mixture back into saucepan. Cook over low heat until thickened, stirring constantly.

5. Spoon custard into crust. Cool to room temperature; refrigerate 3 hours or until set. Arrange blackberries over custard.

Pie Pastry: Combine 1¼ cups all-purpose flour, ¼ teaspoon baking powder and ⅛ teaspoon salt in large bowl. Add ¼ cup vegetable or canola oil and 2 tablespoons milk; stir until blended. Add additional milk, 1 teaspoon at a time, stirring just until dough comes together. Shape dough into a ball.

Strawberry Rhubarb Pie

MAKES 8 SERVINGS

Double Crust Pie Pastry (recipe follows)

1½ cups sugar

½ cup cornstarch

2 tablespoons quick-cooking tapioca

1 tablespoon grated lemon peel

¼ teaspoon ground allspice

4 cups sliced rhubarb (1-inch pieces)

3 cups sliced fresh strawberries

1 egg, lightly beaten

1. Prepare Double Crust Pie Pastry.

2. Preheat oven to 425°F. Roll out one disc pastry into 11-inch circle on floured surface. Line 9-inch pie plate with pastry.

3. Combine sugar, cornstarch, tapioca, lemon peel and allspice in large bowl. Add rhubarb and strawberries; toss to coat.

4. Roll out remaining pastry disc into 10-inch circle. Cut into ½-inch-wide strips with sharp knife.

5. Spoon fruit mixture into crust. Arrange pastry strips in lattice design over fruit. Tuck ends of strips under edge of bottom crust; seal and flute edge. Brush pastry with beaten egg.

6. Bake 50 minutes or until filling is thick and bubbly and crust is golden brown. Remove to wire rack. Serve warm or at room temperature.

Double Crust Pie Pastry: Combine 2½ cups all-purpose flour, 1 teaspoon salt and 1 teaspoon sugar in large bowl. Cut in 1 cup (2 sticks) cold cubed butter with pastry blender or two knives until mixture resembles coarse crumbs. Drizzle with ⅓ cup water, 2 tablespoons at a time, stirring just until dough comes together. Divide dough in half. Shape each half into a disc; wrap with plastic wrap. Refrigerate 30 minutes.

Handheld Apple Pies

MAKES 12 SERVINGS

2 tablespoons sugar

1 teaspoon ground cinnamon

1 large Granny Smith apple, peeled and coarsely chopped

1 package (14 ounces) refrigerated pie crusts (2 crusts)

1. Preheat oven to 350°F. Line baking sheet with parchment paper. Combine sugar and cinnamon in small bowl.

2. Combine apple and 1 tablespoon cinnamon-sugar in medium bowl; toss to coat.

3. Unroll pie crusts on work surface. Cut out 12 circles with 4-inch round cookie cutter or small bowl. Reserve scraps of dough for decoration, if desired.

4. Place one dough circle on prepared baking sheet. Brush water around edge of dough circle. Place about 2 tablespoons apple mixture on half of crust. Fold dough over filling; press with fork to seal. Repeat with remaining dough circles and apple mixture.

5. Cut out shapes from dough scraps with small cookie cutters, if desired; press onto tops of pies.

6. Bake 20 minutes or until crust is golden brown. Sprinkle remaining cinnamon-sugar over hot pies. Serve warm.

Peach Cherry Pie
MAKES 8 SERVINGS

1 refrigerated pie crust (half of 14-ounce package)

Streusel Topping (recipe follows)

¾ cup granulated sugar

3 tablespoons quick-cooking tapioca

1 teaspoon grated lemon peel

½ teaspoon ground cinnamon

⅛ teaspoon salt

4 cups sliced peaches (about 7 medium)

2 cups Bing cherries, pitted

1 tablespoon lemon juice

2 tablespoons butter, cut into pieces

Vanilla ice cream (optional)

1. Let crust stand at room temperature 15 minutes. Prepare Streusel Topping.

2. Preheat oven to 375°F. Line 9-inch pie plate with crust; flute edge.

3. Combine granulated sugar, tapioca, lemon peel, cinnamon and salt in large bowl. Add peaches, cherries and lemon juice; toss to coat. Spoon into crust; dot with butter. Sprinkle with Streusel Topping.

4. Bake 40 minutes or until bubbly. Cool 15 minutes on wire rack. Serve warm or at room temperature with ice cream, if desired.

Streusel Topping: Combine ¾ cup old-fashioned oats, ⅓ cup all-purpose flour, ⅓ cup packed brown sugar and ¾ teaspoon ground cinnamon in medium bowl. Stir in 4 tablespoons melted butter until mixture resembles coarse crumbs.

Mixed Berry Skillet Pie

MAKES 8 SERVINGS

2   packages (12 ounces each) frozen mixed berries

⅓   cup sugar

3   tablespoons cornstarch

2   teaspoons grated orange peel

¼   teaspoon ground ginger

1   refrigerated pie crust (half of 14-ounce package)

1. Preheat oven to 350°F.

2. Combine berries, sugar, cornstarch, orange peel and ginger in large bowl; toss to coat. Spoon into large cast iron skillet.

3. Roll out pie crust into 12-inch circle. Place over skillet; crimp edge as desired. Cut slits in crust to allow steam to escape.

4. Bake about 1 hour or until crust is golden brown. Let stand 1 hour before slicing.

tip If you don't have a cast iron skillet, you can use another ovenproof skillet or a 9-inch deep dish pie plate.

Easy Strawberry Mousse Pie

MAKES 8 SERVINGS

1 cup boiling water

1 package (4-serving size) strawberry gelatin

2 extra ripe, medium DOLE® Bananas

1 carton (6 ounces) strawberry yogurt

2 cups thawed whipped topping

1 cup DOLE® Frozen Whole or Sliced Strawberries, partially thawed, quartered or sliced

1 (9-inch) prepared pie crust

STIR boiling water into gelatin in medium bowl at least 2 minutes until completely dissolved. Place in freezer about 20 minutes or until slightly thickened, stirring occasionally.

PLACE bananas in blender or food processor container. Cover; blend until smooth (1 cup).

COMBINE yogurt and puréed bananas in large bowl. Blend gelatin mixture into banana mixture. Refrigerate until slightly thickened. Fold whipped topping into gelatin mixture with strawberries.

SPOON gelatin mixture into prepared crust. Refrigerate 4 hours or until firm. Garnish with additional whipped topping and strawberries, if desired.

Prep Time: 30 minutes
Chill Time: 4 hours

Simple Fruit Tarts

Sour Cream Apple Tart

MAKES 12 SERVINGS

5 tablespoons butter, divided	½ cup all-purpose flour, divided
¾ cup graham cracker crumbs	2 eggs
1¼ teaspoons ground cinnamon, divided	1 teaspoon vanilla
1⅓ cups sour cream	5 cups coarsely chopped peeled Jonathan apples or other firm red-skinned apples
¾ cup sugar, divided	

1. Preheat oven to 350°F.

2. Melt 3 tablespoons butter in small saucepan over medium heat. Stir in graham cracker crumbs and ¼ teaspoon cinnamon until well blended. Press crumb mixture firmly onto bottom of 9-inch springform pan. Bake 10 minutes. Remove to wire rack to cool.

3. Beat sour cream, ½ cup sugar and 2½ tablespoons flour in large bowl with electric mixer at medium speed until well blended. Beat in eggs and vanilla until well blended. Stir in apples. Spoon mixture into prepared crust.

4. Bake 35 minutes or just until center is set. Remove tart to wire rack. *Turn oven to broil.*

5. Combine remaining 1 teaspoon cinnamon, ¼ cup sugar and 5½ tablespoons flour in small bowl. Cut in remaining 2 tablespoons butter with pastry blender or two knives until mixture resembles coarse crumbs. Sprinkle over top of tart.

6. Broil 3 to 4 minutes or until topping is golden brown. Let stand 15 minutes before serving.

Very Berry Tart
MAKES 8 SERVINGS

1   cup all-purpose flour

5   tablespoons Demerara cane
    sugar,* divided

5   tablespoons cold butter,
    cut into pieces

¼   teaspoon salt

4   tablespoons ice water, divided

½   teaspoon almond extract

1   cup fresh or frozen sliced peeled
    peaches

1   cup fresh or frozen blackberries

½   cup fresh or frozen blueberries

1   tablespoon cornstarch

2   teaspoons orange peel

1   egg yolk

2   tablespoons slivered almonds

*Or substitute turbinado sugar.

1. Combine flour, 2 tablespoons sugar, butter and salt in food processor; process 1 minute or until crumbly. Slowly drizzle in 3 tablespoons water and almond extract; process 30 seconds to 1 minute or until mixture forms a ball. Wrap dough with plastic wrap; refrigerate 1 to 2 hours.

2. Preheat oven to 400°F. Line baking sheet with parchment paper. Roll out dough to ⅛-inch thickness on lightly floured surface; place on prepared baking sheet. Fold in edge of crust about 1 inch.

3. Combine peaches, blackberries, blueberries, remaining 3 tablespoons sugar, cornstarch and orange peel in medium bowl; toss to coat. Drain excess liquid. Mound mixture in center of dough.

4. Whisk egg yolk and remaining 1 tablespoon water in small bowl; brush over edge of dough. Sprinkle with almonds.

5. Bake 20 to 30 minutes or until crust is lightly browned. Remove to wire rack to cool slightly. Serve warm or at room temperature.

Lemon Tart

MARKES 8 TO 10 SERVINGS

1 refrigerated pie crust (half of
  14-ounce package)

5 eggs

1 tablespoon cornstarch

1 cup sugar

½ cup (1 stick) butter

½ cup lemon juice

1. Position rack in center of oven. Preheat oven to 450°F.

2. Line 9-inch tart pan with pie crust, pressing to fit securely against side of pan. Trim off any excess crust. Prick bottom and side of crust with fork.

3. Bake 9 to 10 minutes or until golden brown. Remove to wire rack to cool completely. *Reduce oven temperature to 350°F.*

4. Meanwhile, whisk eggs and cornstarch in medium bowl. Combine sugar, butter and lemon juice in small saucepan; cook and stir over medium-low heat just until butter melts. Whisk in egg mixture; cook 8 to 10 minutes or until thickened, stirring constantly. (Do not let mixture come to a boil.) Pour into medium bowl; stir 1 minute or until cooled slightly. Let cool 10 minutes.

5. Pour cooled lemon curd into baked crust. Bake 25 to 30 minutes or until set. Cool completely before slicing. Store leftovers in refrigerator.

Individual Apple Tarts

MAKES 5 TARTS

1 tablespoon butter

4 medium Granny Smith, Crispin or other firm-fleshed apples, peeled and cut into ¾-inch chunks (about 4 cups)

6 tablespoons granulated sugar

½ teaspoon ground cinnamon

⅛ teaspoon salt

2 teaspoons cornstarch

2 teaspoons lemon juice

1 refrigerated pie crust (half of 14-ounce package)

1 egg, beaten

1 tablespoon coarse or granulated sugar

1. Melt butter in medium saucepan over medium heat; stir in apples, granulated sugar, cinnamon and salt. Cook 10 minutes or until apples are tender, stirring occasionally. Drain apples in colander set over medium bowl; pour liquid back into saucepan. Cook over medium-high heat until liquid is slightly syrupy and reduced by half. Stir in cornstarch; cook 1 minute.

2. Combine apples, lemon juice and cornstarch mixture in medium bowl; toss to coat. Let cool to room temperature.

3. Preheat oven to 425°F. Line large rimmed baking sheet with parchment paper. Unroll pie crust on work surface; cut out five circles with 4-inch round cookie cutter. Place dough circles on prepared baking sheet.

4. Divide apples evenly among dough circles, piling apples in center of each circle and leaving ½-inch border. Fold edges of dough up over filling, overlapping and pleating dough as necessary. Press dough gently to adhere to filling. Brush dough lightly with beaten egg; sprinkle with coarse sugar.

5. Bake about 25 minutes or until crusts are golden brown. Cool on wire rack.

Fabulous Fruit Tart

MAKES 8 SERVINGS

1 refrigerated pie crust (half of 14-ounce package)

1 package (8 ounces) cream cheese, softened

⅓ cup raspberry fruit spread

½ cup sliced nectarines or peaches*

⅓ cup fresh strawberry halves*

½ cup kiwi slices*

⅓ cup fresh blueberries*

3 tablespoons apricot pourable fruit**

2 teaspoons raspberry-flavored liqueur (optional)

*Sliced bananas, plums or raspberries can be substituted.

**Or substitute 2 tablespoons apricot fruit spread combined with 1 tablespoon warm water.

1. Preheat oven to 350°F. Roll out pastry into 12-inch circle; press into 10-inch tart pan with removable bottom or 10-inch quiche dish. Prick bottom and sides of pastry with fork.

2. Bake 18 to 20 minutes or until golden brown. Remove to wire rack to cool completely.

3. Combine cream cheese and fruit spread in medium bowl; mix well. Spread over cooled crust. Refrigerate at least 1 hour.

4. Just before serving, arrange fruit over cream cheese layer. Combine pourable fruit and liqueur, if desired; brush evenly over fruit.

Blueberry Pear Tart

MAKES 8 SERVINGS

1 refrigerated pie crust (half of 14-ounce package)

1 medium ripe pear, peeled and thinly sliced

8 ounces fresh or thawed frozen blueberries or blackberries

⅓ cup raspberry fruit spread

½ teaspoon grated fresh ginger

1. Preheat oven to 450°F.

2. Spray 9-inch tart pan with nonstick cooking spray. Place pie crust in pan; press into bottom and up side of pan to form ½-inch edge. Trim edge. Prick dough several times with fork. Bake 12 minutes. Cool completely in pan on wire rack.

3. Arrange pear slices on bottom of cooled crust; top with blueberries.

4. Place fruit spread in small microwavable bowl. Cover and microwave on HIGH 15 seconds; stir. Repeat, if necessary, until spread is melted. Stir in ginger until blended. Let stand 30 seconds to thicken slightly. Pour over fruit in crust. Refrigerate 2 hours before serving.

Rhubarb Tart

MAKES 8 SERVINGS

1 refrigerated pie crust (half of 14-ounce package)

4 cups sliced rhubarb (½-inch pieces)

1¼ cups sugar

¼ cup all-purpose flour

2 tablespoons butter, cut into small pieces

¼ cup old-fashioned oats

1. Preheat oven to 450°F. Line 9-inch pie plate with crust. Trim excess crust; flute or crimp edge.

2. Combine rhubarb, sugar and flour in medium bowl; toss to coat. Spoon into crust. Dot with butter; sprinkle with oats.

3. Bake 10 minutes. *Reduce oven temperature to 350°F.* Bake 40 minutes or until filling is bubbly and crust is golden brown.

tip When purchasing rhubarb, look for good-sized, crisp, firm stalks that are brightly colored. Avoid any with dried out or brown ends or ones that look limp, fibrous or stringy—these are past their prime. Store rhubarb in a plastic bag in the refrigerator for up to 5 days.

Apple Galette

MAKES 8 SERVINGS

REYNOLDS® Parchment Paper

1 refrigerated pie crust (14-ounce package) or your favorite single crust recipe

5 Granny Smith Apples (about 2 pounds), peeled, cored and thinly sliced

¾ cup packed light brown sugar

2 tablespoons flour

1 teaspoon ground cinnamon

¼ teaspoon ground nutmeg

¼ cup chopped pecans

1 tablespoon butter, cut into small pieces

2 teaspoons milk

Granulated sugar

REYNOLDS Wrap® Aluminum Foil

Preheat oven to 400°F. Place a 14-inch sheet of REYNOLDS® Parchment Paper on counter; sprinkle lightly with flour. Center pie dough on parchment; roll into a 12-inch circle.

Combine apples, brown sugar, flour, cinnamon and nutmeg in large bowl. Spoon apple filling into center of dough, leaving a 2-inch border uncovered. Sprinkle filling with pecans; top with butter. Use parchment paper to lift pie crust border up over filling, pleating edges and leaving an opening in center.

Place Galette on parchment paper on rimmed cookie sheet. Press dough together to seal any cracks to prevent juices from leaking during baking. Brush dough lightly with milk; sprinkle with sugar.

Bake 30 minutes or until crust is golden brown. Cover Galette with REYNOLDS WRAP® Aluminum Foil to prevent overbrowning. Continue baking 5 to 10 minutes longer until juices bubble and apples are tender. Cool 15 minutes. Serve warm, if desired.

Reynolds Kitchens Tips: Be sure to use a cookie sheet with sides. This will prevent any juices that might leak during baking from dripping onto your oven.

Tip: Golden Delicious apples are a great substitute for this recipe.

Prep Time: 25 minutes
Cook Time: 35 minutes

Apricot Tartlets

MAKES 4 TARTLETS

4   sheets frozen phyllo dough, thawed

1   can (15 ounces) apricot halves in juice, drained

4   tablespoons apricot preserves

1   tablespoon powdered sugar

1   teaspoon ground cinnamon

1. Preheat oven to 350°F. Line baking sheet with foil; spray foil with nonstick cooking spray.

2. Place one sheet of phyllo dough on work surface; keep remaining sheets covered with plastic wrap and damp towel. Spray phyllo dough with nonstick cooking spray. Fold in half to create 8×6-inch rectangle; spray with cooking spray.

3. Place 3 apricot halves, cut side up, in center of phyllo dough. Spread with 1 tablespoon preserves. Fold and pleat about 1 inch of dough around edge to form round tartlet shell. Repeat with remaining ingredients to form three more tartlets. Place on prepared baking sheet.

4. Bake 22 minutes or until golden brown and crisp. Combine powdered sugar and cinnamon in small bowl; sprinkle over tartlets. Serve warm.

tip Phyllo dough dries out very quickly and crumbles easily. Keep the thawed phyllo dough wrapped or covered until all the ingredients are assembled and you are ready to work with the dough.

Rustic Plum Tart

MAKES 8 SERVINGS

¼ cup (½ stick) plus 1 tablespoon butter, divided

6 medium plums, each cut into 8 slices (about 3 cups)

¼ cup granulated sugar

½ cup all-purpose flour

½ cup old-fashioned or quick oats

¼ cup packed brown sugar

½ teaspoon ground cinnamon

¼ teaspoon salt

1 egg

1 teaspoon water

1 refrigerated pie crust (half of 14-ounce package)

1 tablespoon chopped crystallized ginger

1. Preheat oven to 425°F. Line baking sheet with parchment paper.

2. Melt 1 tablespoon butter in large skillet over high heat. Add plums; cook and stir 3 minutes or until softened. Stir in granulated sugar; cook 1 minute or until juices are thickened. Remove from heat; set aside.

3. Combine flour, oats, brown sugar, cinnamon and salt in medium bowl. Cut in remaining ¼ cup butter with pastry blender or two knives until mixture resembles coarse crumbs.

4. Beat egg and water in small bowl. Unroll pie crust on prepared baking sheet. Brush lightly with egg mixture. Sprinkle with ¼ cup oat mixture, leaving 2-inch border around edge of crust. Spoon plums over oat mixture, leaving juices in skillet. Sprinkle with ginger. Fold crust edge up around plums, overlapping as necessary. Sprinkle with remaining oat mixture. Brush edge of crust with egg mixture.

5. Bake 25 minutes or until crust is golden brown. Cool slightly before serving.

Fun Fruit Desserts

Blueberry Shortcakes

MAKES 12 SHORTCAKES

Shortcakes

- 2 cups all-purpose flour
- ½ cup packed brown sugar
- 4 teaspoons baking powder
- ¼ teaspoon grated nutmeg
- ½ cup (1 stick) cold butter, cut into pieces
- ½ cup plus 1 tablespoon milk, divided
- 1 egg, at room temperature
- 1 teaspoon vanilla

Filling

- 1 cup whipped topping
- 2 teaspoons packed brown sugar
- 2 pints fresh blueberries

1. Position rack in center of oven. Preheat oven to 400°F. Line baking sheet with parchment paper.

2. Combine flour, ½ cup brown sugar, baking powder and nutmeg in food processor; pulse to blend. Add butter; pulse 30 seconds or until mixture is crumbly and butter is in pea-sized pieces.

3. Whisk ½ cup milk, egg and vanilla in 2-cup measure until well blended. With motor running, pour milk mixture through feed tube; process about 30 seconds or until moist dough forms.

4. Turn out dough onto large piece of waxed paper dusted with flour. Press dough into circle about ½ inch thick with floured hands. Cut dough with 2¼-inch round biscuit cutter; place 2 inches apart on prepared baking sheet. Gather scraps; knead lightly. Repeat process to make 12 rounds. Brush dough with remaining 1 tablespoon milk.

5. Bake 12 to 15 minutes or until light golden. Remove to wire rack to cool completely.

6. Combine whipped topping and 2 teaspoons brown sugar in medium bowl; mix well. Split shortcakes; fill with whipped cream mixture and blueberries. Serve immediately.

Peach Turnovers

MAKES 6 SERVINGS

2 cups chopped peeled fresh peaches or frozen sliced peaches, thawed, drained and chopped

2 tablespoons granulated sugar

1 tablespoon all-purpose flour

¼ teaspoon vanilla

⅛ teaspoon ground nutmeg

6 sheets frozen phyllo dough, thawed

1 tablespoon powdered sugar

1. Preheat oven to 375°F. Line large baking sheet with parchment paper. Combine peaches, granulated sugar, flour, vanilla and nutmeg in medium bowl; toss to coat.

2. Place one sheet of phyllo dough on work surface. (Keep remaining dough covered.) Lightly spray dough with nonstick cooking spray. Top with second sheet of phyllo. Using sharp knife or pizza cutter, cut lengthwise into two strips, each about 12×4 inches.

3. Spoon about ⅓ cup peach mixture onto each dough strip about 1 inch from end. Fold one corner over filling to make triangle. Continue folding as you would fold a flag to form triangle that encloses filling. Repeat with remaining dough and filling. Place on prepared baking sheet. Lightly spray tops of turnovers with cooking spray.

4. Bake about 17 minutes or until golden brown. Remove to wire rack to cool 10 minutes. Sprinkle with powdered sugar. Serve immediately.

Raspberry Clafouti

MAKES 8 TO 10 SERVINGS

3 eggs	½ teaspoon vanilla
⅓ cup sugar	⅔ cup almond flour
1 cup half-and-half	Pinch salt
2 tablespoons butter, melted and slightly cooled	2 containers (6 ounces each) fresh raspberries

1. Preheat oven to 325°F. Generously grease 9-inch ceramic pie plate or tart pan.

2. Beat eggs and sugar in large bowl with electric mixer at medium speed 4 minutes or until slightly thickened. Add half-and-half, butter and vanilla; whisk to combine. Gradually whisk in almond flour and salt. Pour enough batter into prepared pan to just cover bottom. Bake 10 minutes or until set.

3. Remove pan from oven. Scatter raspberries evenly over baked batter. Stir in remaining batter and pour over raspberries.

4. Bake 40 to 45 minutes or until center is set and top is golden brown. Cool completely on wire rack. Refrigerate leftovers.

Note: Clafouti is a rustic French dish that is made by topping fresh fruit with a custard-like batter. The most famous and traditional clafouti is made with cherries, but berries, plums, peaches and pears are also used.

Apple Crêpes
MAKES ABOUT 14 CRÊPES

1 cup rice flour

¼ teaspoon salt

¼ teaspoon ground nutmeg

1 cup half-and-half

3 tablespoons butter, melted, divided

½ teaspoon vanilla

3 eggs

Apple Filling (recipe follows)

1. Combine rice flour, salt and nutmeg in medium bowl. Gradually whisk in half-and-half until smooth. Add 2 tablespoons butter and vanilla. Whisk in eggs, one at a time, until batter is smooth and reaches consistency of heavy cream.

2. Prepare Apple Filling; keep warm.

3. Heat 8- or 9-inch nonstick skillet over medium heat. Brush lightly with remaining 1 tablespoon butter. Pour about ¼ cup batter into center of pan. Immediately pick up pan and swirl to coat with batter. Cook 1 minute or until crêpe is dull on top and edges are dry. Turn and cook 30 seconds. Remove to plate; repeat with remaining batter.

4. Fill crêpes with Apple Filling or other desired fillings. Garnish, if desired.

Apple Filling: Peel 5 firm apples (Granny Smith, Jonathan or Golden Delicious) and cut into ¾-inch slices. Combine apples, ¼ cup dried cranberries, 1 tablespoon sugar and 1 teaspoon ground cinnamon in large bowl; toss to coat. Melt 2 tablespoons butter in large nonstick skillet over medium heat. Add apple mixture; cook and stir 5 minutes or until apples soften.

tip Freeze leftover crêpes between sheets of waxed paper in a large resealable food storage bag.

Mini Strawberry Shortcakes

MAKES 16 MINI SHORTCAKES

1   quart fresh strawberries,
    hulled and sliced

½   cup sugar, divided

1   cup all-purpose flour

2   teaspoons baking powder

¼   teaspoon salt

¼   cup (½ stick) cold butter,
    cut into small pieces

1¼   cups whipping cream,
     divided

1. Combine strawberries and ¼ cup sugar in medium bowl; set aside.

2. Preheat oven to 425°F. Combine flour, 2 tablespoons sugar, baking powder and salt in large bowl; mix well. Cut in butter with pastry blender or two knives until mixture resembles coarse crumbs. Gradually add ½ cup cream, stirring gently until dough comes together. (Dough will be slightly sticky.)

3. Turn out dough onto lightly floured surface; knead gently four to six times. Pat dough into 6-inch square. Cut into 16 (1½-inch) squares with sharp knife. Place 2 inches apart on ungreased baking sheet.

4. Bake about 10 minutes or until golden brown. Remove biscuits to wire rack to cool slightly. Meanwhile, beat remaining ¾ cup cream and 2 tablespoons sugar in medium bowl with electric mixer at high speed until soft peaks form.

5. Split biscuits in half horizontally. Fill with berry mixture and whipped cream. Serve immediately.

Pear & Cranberry Strudel with Caramel Sauce

MAKES 6 SERVINGS

½ of a 17.3-ounce package
     PEPPERIDGE FARM® Puff Pastry
     Sheets (1 sheet)

1 egg

1 tablespoon water

½ cup dried cranberries

½ cup packed brown sugar

2 tablespoons cornstarch

½ teaspoon ground cinnamon

2 large Bosc pears, peeled, cored
    and diced

¾ cup prepared caramel topping

1. Thaw the pastry sheet at room temperature for 40 minutes or until it's easy to handle. Heat the oven to 375°F. Lightly grease or line a baking sheet with parchment paper. Beat the egg and water in a small bowl with a fork.

2. Place the cranberries into a small bowl and pour hot water over them to cover. Let stand for 5 minutes. Drain. Mix the brown sugar, cornstarch and cinnamon in a medium bowl. Add the pears and cranberries and toss to coat.

3. Unroll the pastry sheet on a lightly floured surface. Roll the pastry sheet into a 14×11-inch rectangle. With the long side facing you, spoon the pear mixture onto the lower third of the pastry. Starting at the long side, roll up like a jelly roll. Tuck the ends under to seal. Place seam-side down on the baking sheet. Brush with the egg mixture. Cut several 2-inch-long slits 2 inches apart on the top.

4. Bake for 25 minutes or until the strudel is golden. Cool on the baking sheet on a wire rack for 15 minutes. Heat the caramel topping according to the package directions and serve with the strudel.

Kitchen Tip: Prepare the strudel through Step 3 and refrigerate for up to 24 hours or freeze.

Fruit-Filled Cream Puffs

MAKES 10 SERVINGS

1 cup water

⅓ cup canola oil

2 tablespoons sugar

¼ teaspoon salt

1 cup all-purpose flour

2 eggs

2 egg whites

1¾ cups milk

1 package (4-serving size) vanilla instant pudding and pie filling mix

2 cups fresh berries, such as sliced strawberries, raspberries or blueberries

1. Preheat oven to 400°F. Line large baking sheet with parchment paper.

2. Combine water, oil, sugar and salt to a boil in medium saucepan; bring to a boil over medium heat. Add flour all at once, stirring vigorously until dough pulls away from side of pan (about 1 minute). Immediately remove from heat; cool at least 5 minutes.

3. Add eggs and egg whites, one at a time, beating with spoon or whisk after each addition, until completely incorporated. Drop dough by scant ¼ cupfuls into 10 mounds about 3 inches apart onto prepared baking sheet.

4. Bake 30 to 35 minutes or until dry and golden brown. Remove to wire rack to cool completely. Meanwhile, whisk milk and pudding mix in medium bowl about 2 minutes or until thickened.

5. Cut off top third of each cream puff and remove any strands of soft dough. Fill bottoms with pudding and berries; replace tops. Serve immediately or cover and refrigerate until ready to serve.

Acknowledgments

The publisher would like to thank the companies listed below
for the use of their recipes and photographs in this publication.

ACH Food Companies, Inc.

Campbell Soup Company

Cream of Wheat® Cereal, A Division of B&G Foods North America, Inc.

Dole Food Company, Inc.

Recipe courtesy of the Reynolds Kitchens

Unilever

Metric Conversion Chart

VOLUME MEASUREMENTS (dry)

1/8 teaspoon = 0.5 mL
1/4 teaspoon = 1 mL
1/2 teaspoon = 2 mL
3/4 teaspoon = 4 mL
1 teaspoon = 5 mL
1 tablespoon = 15 mL
2 tablespoons = 30 mL
1/4 cup = 60 mL
1/3 cup = 75 mL
1/2 cup = 125 mL
2/3 cup = 150 mL
3/4 cup = 175 mL
1 cup = 250 mL
2 cups = 1 pint = 500 mL
3 cups = 750 mL
4 cups = 1 quart = 1 L

VOLUME MEASUREMENTS (fluid)

1 fluid ounce (2 tablespoons) = 30 mL
4 fluid ounces (1/2 cup) = 125 mL
8 fluid ounces (1 cup) = 250 mL
12 fluid ounces (1 1/2 cups) = 375 mL
16 fluid ounces (2 cups) = 500 mL

WEIGHTS (mass)

1/2 ounce = 15 g
1 ounce = 30 g
3 ounces = 90 g
4 ounces = 120 g
8 ounces = 225 g
10 ounces = 285 g
12 ounces = 360 g
16 ounces = 1 pound = 450 g

DIMENSIONS

1/16 inch = 2 mm
1/8 inch = 3 mm
1/4 inch = 6 mm
1/2 inch = 1.5 cm
3/4 inch = 2 cm
1 inch = 2.5 cm

OVEN TEMPERATURES

250°F = 120°C
275°F = 140°C
300°F = 150°C
325°F = 160°C
350°F = 180°C
375°F = 190°C
400°F = 200°C
425°F = 220°C
450°F = 230°C

BAKING PAN SIZES

Utensil	Size in Inches/Quarts	Metric Volume	Size in Centimeters
Baking or	8×8×2	2 L	20×20×5
Cake Pan	9×9×2	2.5 L	23×23×5
(square or	12×8×2	3 L	30×20×5
rectangular)	13×9×2	3.5 L	33×23×5
Loaf Pan	8×4×3	1.5 L	20×10×7
	9×5×3	2 L	23×13×7
Round Layer	8×1½	1.2 L	20×4
Cake Pan	9×1½	1.5 L	23×4
Pie Plate	8×1¼	750 mL	20×3
	9×1¼	1 L	23×3
Baking Dish	1 quart	1 L	—
or Casserole	1½ quart	1.5 L	—
	2 quart	2 L	—